Hi welcome to my classroom. Come in and take a seat. In this book you will be equipped with the knowledge and tools necessary for planning recovering from or maintaining a Brazilian butt lift procedure. After each lesson you will level up on your way to becoming your very own BBL expert. I hope enjoy learning as much as I like teaching.

Egypt

In recent years, there has been a massive growth in popularity of the Brazilian Butt Lift (BBL) surgery, sometimes referred to as a fat transfer. This surgery is comprised of liposuction (removal of fat) from various parts of the body. The fat is then cleaned and injected into the buttocks through the use of cannulas.

This procedure changes the shape, size, and fullness of the butt. Many people choose to undergo this surgery for various reasons. However, deciding on this procedure is a life altering commitment. Unlike buying a dress, it cannot be returned. There is no "WRONG" reason to get a BBL unless you feel you are being pressured by someone to do so.

Once you have decided to go through with the BBL, be aware that almost everyone in the world has an opinion about undergoing a cosmetic procedure. Be prepared to receive negative criticism or positive support from people you know and those who you do not know. Don't be afraid to be the best version of yourself. Your life is for you to live therefore, do not sacrifice your happiness for anyone. Make the decision you feel is best for you.

Now that you have decided that you would like to undergo a BBL procedure there are a few things you should begin to research. Take full body pictures to show your normal dimensions. You should have visuals of your body from a multidirectional approach. Take a full frontal, left & right sides, and a few shots of your back. Think of the areas you consider to be "problematic" and would like to change. Now create an idea of how you would like to look, post surgery. Think about if you would prefer a more natural looking figure with hips, or if you would like to look more like a curvy vixen with lats. Do you want more fullness at the top of your butt which creates a shelf? Or do you want a slope where the most fullness of your butt is towards the bottom? Look at your starting point and try to set realistic goals depending on your foundation, height and weight.

Keep in mind that the surgery will have some limitations on how much fat can be removed from your body in one surgical procedure. Depending on the look you desire, you may need to undergo several rounds of the surgery to achieve that look.

It is a great idea to have pictures so you can show your doctor a visual of your vision for your body. "Wish pics" can be gathered from all over the internet, social media, or maybe even someone you know. Wish pics are pictures of people whose body you admire. They are not necessary, but many people feel better having them handy as a reference point when consulting with their potential doctor.

Figure Out Your Price Range

Since a Brazilian Butt Lift is an elective surgery your medical insurance will not cover it. This means you will have to pay out of pocket for all of your expenses. Consider how much money you are willing or able to invest in this procedure. Consider when you want to have the procedure done. Some doctors have a standard fixed price, while others offer seasonal promotions and price cuts. You will also need to factor in your travel expenses should you choose a doctor in another state or country.

No matter where you have surgery cash is always a form of payment accepted by any clinic. At some clinics it may be the ONLY form of payment accepted, although some clinics take debit or credit cards. Your clinic should inform you of accepted payment options when you decide to book your procedure.

Do you want to pay for it all at once or take out a loan? If paying for it all at once is not an option you may want to finance your procedure. The same way you can put a down payment on a car or house, now you can put a down payment on your butt. Financing allows you to make small payments overtime. There is normally a down payment fee required upfront which is a small percentage of the total cost of the procedure. Some clinics have "in-house" financing which do not require credit checks and you pay the clinic directly according to the pay schedule you create. With in-house financing, most clinics require the balance to be paid in full before your surgery is performed. If you finance through a company you can have your surgery now and pay for it later. CareCredit and Alphaeon are amongst some of the most popular companies used by clinics for cosmetic surgery. Another way to finance is applying for a loan through either your bank or a loan company. If your credit score does not meet their standards then you may need a co-signer to be approved. Getting a BBL will cost thousands of dollars plus additional fees. If you choose not to go the financing route you might have to make some sacrifices to fund your surgery.

Start by making some lifestyle changes. Make a list of your monthly expenses and see if there are any areas where you can save or cut back. You may also want to consider looking for an extra source of income. There are money making opportunities all around you so be on the lookout for them. Below is an example of a monthly budget:

Monthly Budget

MONEY IN	
Paycheck	$5,000
Additional income	$800
TOTAL INCOME	$5,800

MONEY OUT	
Housing (Rent, mortgage, taxes, insurance)	$1,500
Utilities (Electricity, water, gas)	$150
Car Payment/Car Insurance	$400
Phone Bill	$200
Groceries	$400
Wifi	$50
Credit Card	$50
Savings/Emergency fund	$500
Misc (Movies, dinner, girls, night etc.)	$300
TOTAL EXPENSES	$3,550

MONEY LEFT OVER	
Income minus expenses	$2,250

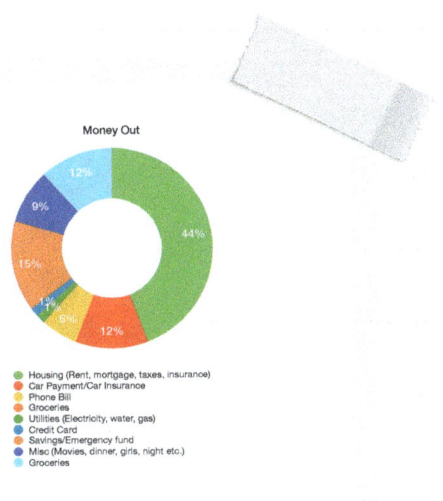

Surgery Location

Where would you like to have surgery? Within the United States or abroad? Think about where you would be most comfortable having surgery, and where it is most convenient for you. In your country or another country? In the state you reside in or another state? This helps you to narrow in on doctors within a specific area. Some people travel outside of where they live because they may have seen a doctor's work which they like. If you choose to go out of the country even if a doctor is board certified, the standards may vary from those in your home country.

Finding A Doctor

Now that you have a body goal in mind and know your price range, it is time to find a doctor who can successfully fulfill your vision. Safety is the number one rule when choosing a surgeon. Find a doctor that has credentials (board-certified), and can safely perform the surgery. The ideal is to search for a doctor with no or a low patient death ratio. This is very important.

Keep in mind that everyone has a specialty and some doctors may deliver better results working on larger or smaller framed people. Look into obtaining a surgeon with experience that delivers consistent results. Instagram is a popular tool surgeons use to showcase their work. Try searching for doctors by using tags/hashtags (#). Search BBL plus the city, state or country you are considering. For example: BBLMiami or #BBLMiami. Realself.com is another popular tool used to aid in locating a doctor. When you see a doctor that you like don't rush things out of eagerness, give it time! Take time and research them, talk to previous patients and even reach out to them or their team with any concerns. Most importantly, choose the surgeon that you feel will give you the best results you will be happy with.

Virtual Consultation or In person Wanted Required

There are two ways to consult with your doctor to confirm if you are a great candidate for a BBL. Initially, it will be either a virtual or in person appointment. If you are a local it is more convenient to have an in person consultation. If you are not local of your potential doctor, then a virtual consultation will be performed.

For a virtual consultation the doctor or surgical coordinator will send you a questionnaire which you will be required to complete and return along with pictures of your body. Some doctors use virtual calling apps such as skype for consultations. Some doctors require an in-person consultation whether you are a local or not. If that is the case with a doctor you are seriously considering then you will have to factor in additional travel fees and hotel costs.

Transportation Fees

Once you find a doctor think about how you will get there. Is the clinic within driving distance or will you have to fly to get there? Plane ticket prices fluctuate often, and it will most likely be cheaper to purchase your tickets a few months to 6 weeks in advance. The cheapest days to fly are Tuesday, Wednesday, and Saturday. The cheapest times to fly are early morning, mid day, and the end of the work day. It is okay to use websites that compare prices for different airlines, but it is best to check each airline website individually as some flights may not show up on some websites. Ticket prices may even be cheaper at the airport counter (when booking in advance) so go in and inquire.

Think about what items you will need to take and how large of a suitcase you will need. Check with the airline to see how many carry-on and checked bags are complimentary or if you will have to pay for luggage. If so, this is an additional fee added onto the price of the plane ticket. When purchasing your tickets be sure to book larger seats on returning flights. You will still be swollen and will have to sit with a pillow so a larger seat may make your flight more comfortable. If you are able to book a first class ticket for the way back it is advised to do so, especially if you have a longer flight.

If you choose to drive to the doctor then consider the miles you will have to drive, how many miles your vehicle gets per gallon, and the price of gas. My suggestion is to NOT plan on driving yourself back home or to a hotel after the surgery is performed. Someone else should be doing all the driving for you. Remember, you do not want to put any pressure on your bottom until you are given the green light to do so. You will be in pain coming out of the surgery and the sooner you can reach a bed to rest the better your body will feel.

Time Off From Work

Think about how many days you can afford to miss from school or work. If you have vacation days, consider using them right before a time period that you might have extra time off due to the holidays. For example, spring break, summer break, or winter break are the perfect times. Thus, you will need to consult with your surgeon to find out how many days they require for you to stay local after your operation. Some doctors require a minimum of 3 days while others require as many as 21 days. This will help you factor in how many days you will need to take off from school or work.

If you are traveling far you may want to get there a few days before your surgery, because you will have preoperative appointments. Also, you may want to explore the city before your surgery especially, since you will have limited mobility afterwards. For patients traveling abroad, most doctors require you to arrive 72 hours before surgery. Although everyone heals at different rates the average recovery period for a BBL is typically 2 weeks. You may feel well enough to return to work within a week, but I would recommend that you take at least 2 weeks off from everything. Even though the BBL is a common procedure it is still a form of surgery. Do not underestimate the power of R-E-S-T. It is the body's way of healing itself.

Recovery Home Prices and Amenities

After surgery you will need a place to recover. Most people choose to stay in a recovery home. A recovery home is like a hotel with nurses and nursing assistants who are on call to assist you with the things you will need help with. Most recovery homes provide drop-off/pick-up services for patients on the day of surgery and take you to any follow-up appointments.

They also make sure you have 3 meals and snacks daily for the duration of your stay. Some recovery homes have an all-inclusive deal which includes lymphatic drainage massages. Other recovery homes may offer them at an additional fee. The price of recovery homes varies based on its location and the duration of your stay. This will be an additional fee you will have to pay aside from the BBL surgery. Know your preferences and plan for what will work for you. Some doctors offer surgery packages that include a recovery home. Some recovery homes give discounts for patients from certain doctors/clinics. Most recovery homes do not allow additional people to stay with you however, the ones that do will charge additional fees for any non-patients.

When choosing a recovery home check for reviews on customer service, cleanliness, and any amenities you may be interested in. Speak to someone that has been to the home and try to obtain their honest feedback. Do not be afraid to ask questions after all this will be your home for the next few days! Some people decide against recovery homes and book hotels or Airbnb's. If you decide to do so, you will need to arrange to have a travel nurse, transportation, and someone to help you with food and other things you will need.

Lymphatic Massages

After liposuction you will need lymphatic drainage massages. These massages help to eliminate the excess fluid from your body. They also help to combat and ease the pain from swelling. Although you might experience some discomfort during a lymphatic massage, afterwards you will be glad you had them. The price of a lymphatic massage varies based on location. Your clinic or recovery home may provide your initial massages for you while you are required to pay for additional massages.

Another option is finding a lymphatic massage specialist that travels to you. In the early stages after surgery it is best that you get a massage until all of the fluid has been drained. Some patients get as little as 3 massages while others may get as many as 7-10. Ask your doctor how many massages is recommended for you. The amount of massages needed may vary on a case by case basis.

Labs To Complete

Before your surgery can be performed your doctor or surgical coordinator will send you a list of labs that you are required to take. This practice is implemented in order to ensure that you are in good health and able to be operated on without any complications. These labs must be taken no earlier than 30 days before your operation, and must be turned in to your surgeon at least 2 weeks before your procedure. Your surgeon will give you the exact deadlines.

Consult with your primary care physician's office to see if they can administer or give you referrals for any of your required labs. Third parties include Urgent Care Centers, LabCorp, Quest Diagnostics etc. If your insurance does not cover the cost of your labs, you will have to pay out of pocket. You could pay an estimated fee of $200-$600 for your labs so be prepared to cover any additional costs. To cut costs and save money try to find local places within your area that do free lab testing for some of your labs.

The list of labs will include the following:

- HIV
- HCG Quantitative (Pregnancy test)
- Basic Metabolic
- CBC (Complete Blood Count) with Platelets
- PT/INR/APTT
- EKG
- Medical clearance (letter from your PCP stating BMI, allergies, medical conditions, family medical history, and vitals saying you are LOW RISK for surgery based on your lab results).

These are the basic required labs but your doctor may require more specific to your case. A word of advice is to be completely honest about your medical history with your PCP, and surgeon. Do not be so desperate to have the procedure done that you neglect to disclose pertinent medical information to them. Your life could depend on it.

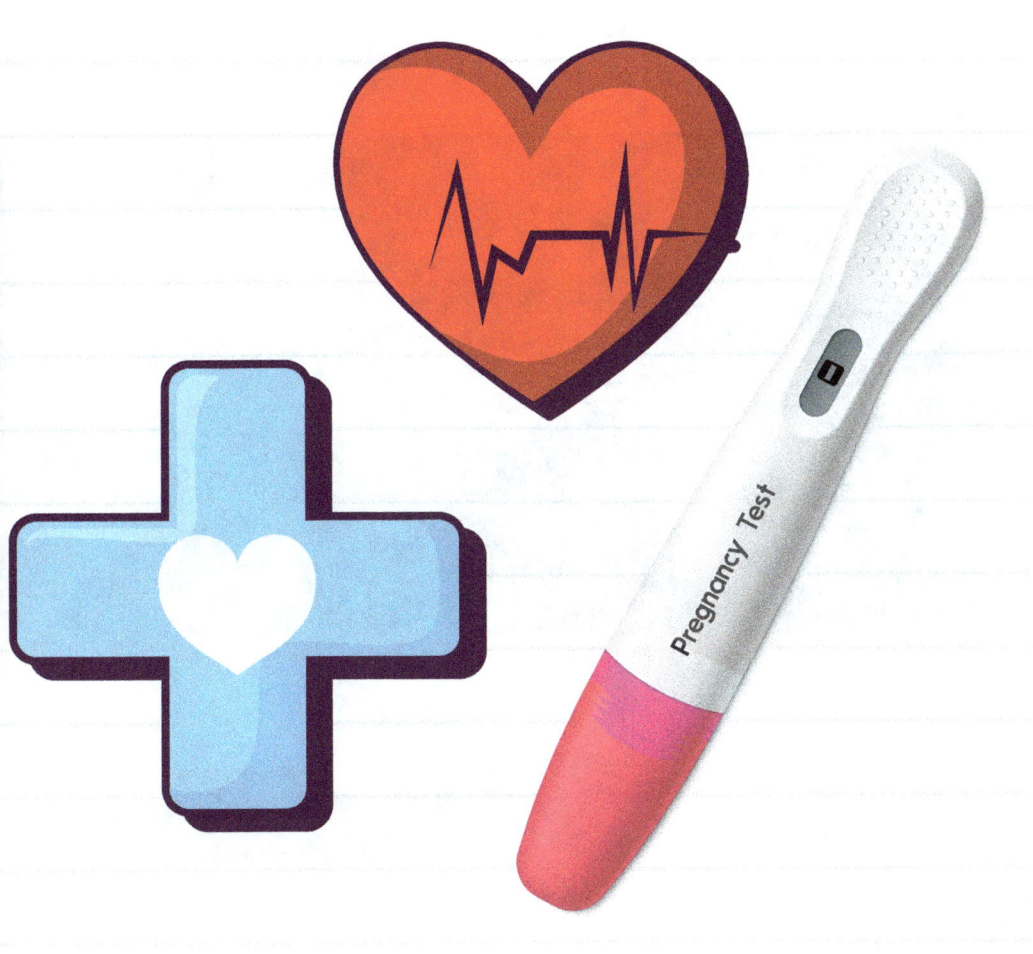

Before surgery your doctor/surgical coordinator will give you a list of vitamins and supplements that you may want to take or avoid. It is imperative that you follow these instructions and do not take any items on the "avoid" list so that you can reduce your chances of any complications post-op.

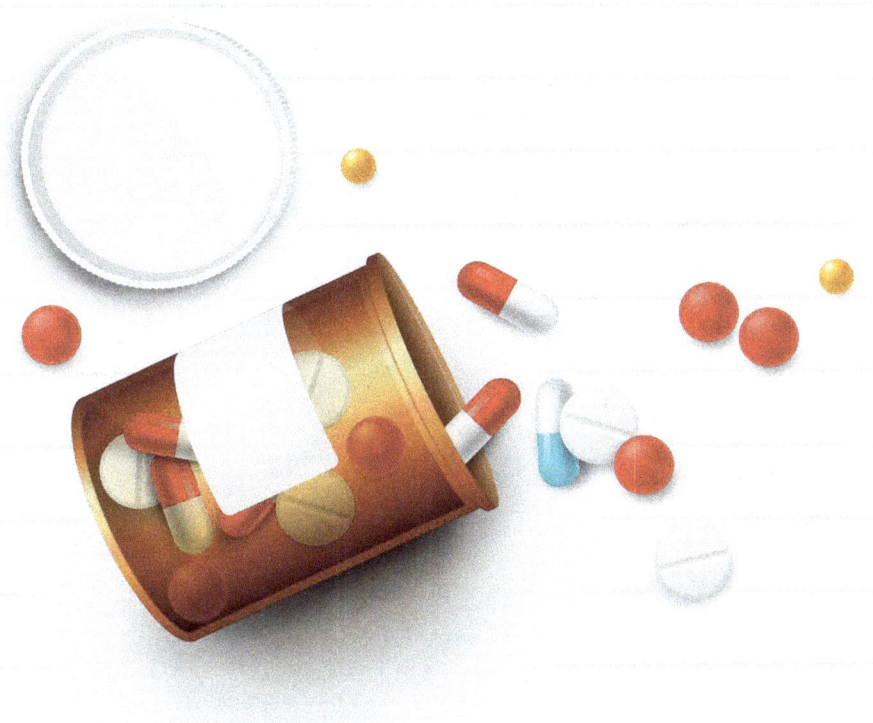

Items Needed

In order to make things flow smoother for yourself after surgery you should make sure to have the necessary supplies ahead of time. Below is a list of supplies. Your surgeon will give you a prescription for a few medications at your pre-op appointment. Among those medications will be your pain medication. Make sure that you have someone to fill your prescriptions asap and that they bring your pain medicine when they come to pick you up!

- ☐ Prescription medication (pain, antibiotics, anti-nausea)
- ☐ Arnica gel, salve or cream.
- ☐ Arnica tea
- ☐ Lipo foams
- ☐ Lumbar molder
- ☐ Abdominal board
- ☐ Chux disposable underpads
- ☐ Female urinal
- ☐ Slip on shoes
- ☐ Hand sanitizer
- ☐ Clorox wipes
- ☐ Toiletries
- ☐ Compression socks
- ☐ Baby wipes
- ☐ Plush bath robe
- ☐ Boppy pillow

- ☐ BBL pillow
- ☐ Maxi pads
- ☐ Stool softener
- ☐ Shower curtain
- ☐ Sheets
- ☐ Muscle roller
- ☐ Antibiotic ointment
- ☐ Scar treatment (gel/cream/tape)
- ☐ Stage 1 faja (low compression)
- ☐ Stage 2 faja (medium — extreme compression)
- ☐ Measuring tape
- ☐ Antibacterial soap
- ☐ Q-tips
- ☐ Extra strength Tylenol
- ☐ Extension cord
- ☐ Gatorade / Pedialyte / Powerade / Coconut Water
- ☐ Water
- ☐ Soup and crackers (for first 24 hours)
- ☐ _____
- ☐ _____
- ☐ _____
- ☐ _____
- ☐ _____
- ☐ _____
- ☐ _____
- ☐ _____
- ☐ _____

Arrangements for Postop Care

Before you have surgery you should know the who, what, and where's. Who will be taking you to surgery and who will be picking you up? Will you be staying at a recovery home, with friends/family, air bnb or a hotel? Who will be performing your lymphatic massages? Who will fill your prescription medication? These arrangements will need to be made and confirmed prior to surgery to aide in keeping your stress levels down, and to ensure your comfort and safety.

24 Hours before surgery

- Do not eat or drink anything after the designated time given to you by your surgeon
- Stay hydrated
- Eat easily digestible foods (pasta, yogurt, pancakes)
- Take a thorough shower and shampoo with the designated products
- DO NOT DO ANY FORM OF DRUGS or ALCOHOL

Waking up early in the morning is a very important part of your surgery day. When you wake up (if you were able to sleep), you will be excited for your big day! Make sure to take out all piercings and remove all jewelry. Your attire should include a warm robe, slip-on shoes and stockings. If you will have a friend, relative, or spouse waiting with you at the clinic you may want to take your phone and headphones or some sort of entertainment while you wait to go into the operating room. If you have recovery home staff with you or you are getting dropped off you might want to leave these items at home to ensure their security. Ultimately, it is best to leave all valuables at home.

If you have high blood pressure make sure to take your medication with a small sip of water before you leave home (if your surgeon has given you the clearance to do so). You do not want your blood pressure too high or too low because it creates a hazard and will put a halt on you having a procedure performed at the scheduled time.

Arrival

You will be given an arrival time at your pre-op appointment, or a coordinator will contact you the night before with an arrival time. Make sure you show up on time to avoid any delays. Most surgeons perform several operations daily and being late can set everyone back. Therefore, I urge you to please be considerate of the surgeon's time and the other patients time.

Waiting Process

Once you arrive at the clinic, you must check in with the receptionist to notify them of your arrival. Once they check you in, you get to play the waiting game. At some point the nurse will check your vital signs (temperature, pulse, respiration, blood pressure & pain level) before you get prepped for surgery. You will also need to give them a urine sample so they can run some last minute tests. You will be placed in a patient's room. There you are given a paper surgical gown, and a hairnet, in which you will have to change into. You should also be given a bag with your name or some sort of identifier in which to place your belongings.

The anesthesiologist will come in and ask you a few questions then he or she will start an IV. Lastly, your surgeon will chat with you briefly while they mark your problem areas in preparation for surgery. This is your time to mention any last minute concerns that you might have, and to re-inform them of the areas you would really like for them to focus on. When it is time to walk into the OR you may be slightly nervous or have some last minute jitters. Walk into the OR mentally prepared for the surgery. Pray and remain positive. Trust that you have made the right decision and are in good hands. Relax, take deep breaths, and keep calm.

Waking Up After Surgery

At most facilities a BBL is an outpatient procedure, which means you do not stay overnight and get to go home the same day. When you awake from the procedure you may be tired and disoriented for a moment or two. These are normal side effects of the anesthesia. You should awake in a recovery room where nurses are monitoring your vital signs. When it is cleared for you to leave, you will be discharged to the person who is picking you up. You will be in pain, so it is best they have your pain medication brought to you at pickup time. Since you will not be able to sit on your butt for the ride home you will have to choose another method. Popular methods are laying across the back seat on your stomach, or kneeling facedown in the passenger seat with the seat reclined as far back as possible. To avoid getting any fluid leakage on the seats, it is best to place a plastic shower curtain or disposable underpad underneath you.

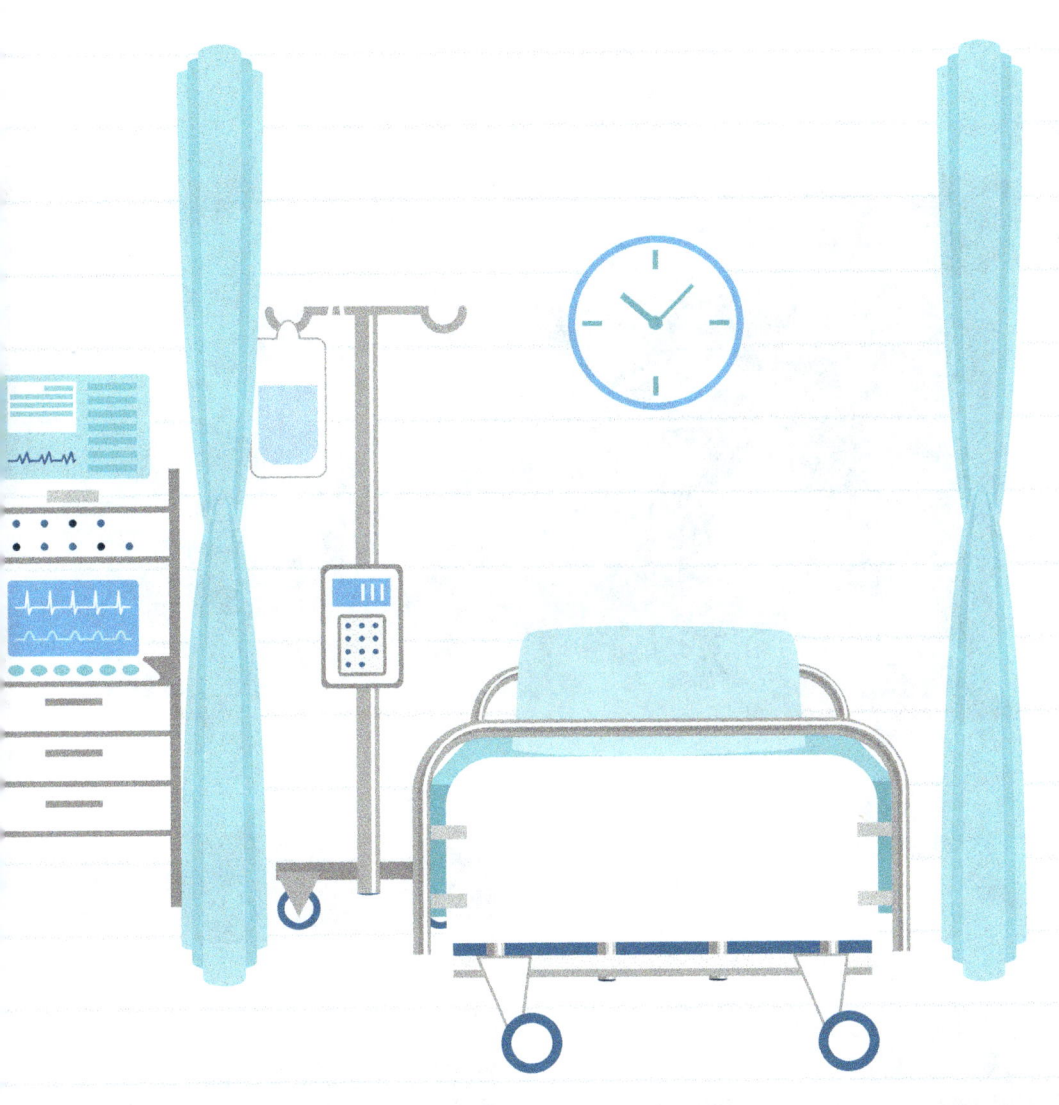

The day of surgery and the first 2-3 days afterwards are when you may experience the most pain and discomfort. You may also have symptoms of nausea, lightheadedness, or dizziness. When getting up take your time so that you will not fall and hurt yourself. It is important to stay hydrated and to eat so that you have energy. Your doctor will give you instructions on what to eat post-surgery. For the first 24 hours after surgery, most doctors recommend you to eat soup, crackers, yogurt, and soft foods. After about 24 hours you should be able to start back eating more solid foods. However, you probably will not have a heavy appetite, so keep your meals lite and well balanced.

Feeding The Fat

Your body will need extra calories since it is working in overdrive to provide a blood supply to your newly transferred fat cells. Keep in mind that your body is recovering from the traumas of surgery. Foods that are dense with nutrients will supply your body with the necessary vitamins and minerals that will help aid its recovery. When feeding the fat try to stay away from processed foods and trans fat.

We are taught not to include much fat in our diet however, not all fat is bad for you. Monounsaturated fats and polyunsaturated fats are referred to as "good fats" because they are good for your cholesterol, heart and overall health. Avocado, salmon, almonds, walnuts, extra virgin olive oil, coconut oil, and grass-fed butter, egg yolks, chia seeds, peanut butter are popular choices of good fats. The best and healthiest way to feed the fat is to consume "good fats" in moderation.

There is a common misconception that after lipo the fat will not come back. If you gain weight after lipo, the remaining fat cells all over your body will enlarge. It may be less noticeable, and you may appear smaller in certain areas of the body due to the decrease in fat cells from the lipo, however it can still go to other areas such as your arms, back, face and more. Some fat can return as toxic fat. Toxic fat grows underneath your muscle and around your organs. This can not be lipoed. Therefore, it is best to maintain a healthy lifestyle and eating habits even after your procedure.

Do Consume	Try to Avoid
Avocados	Margarine
Eggs	French fries
Coconut oil	Doughnuts
Raw nuts and seeds	Cookies
Olive oil	Pastries
Salmon	Crackers
Flaxseed	Processed meats
Leafy green vegetables	Canola oil
Organic butter	Hydrogenated oils
Organic nut oils	
Red meats	
Veggies	
soups	
yogurts	
fruits	

Fajas

After surgery you most likely will be required to wear a special surgical garment which is often referred to as a faja [pronounced fah-hah] or girdle. Fajas usually come in two stages, with stage 1 being little to no compression, and stage 2 providing more compression. Sometimes depending on the model, or brand, there is even a 3rd stage of compression which provides extreme compression and should not be used in the beginning stages of recovery.

Note that every doctor does not recommend wearing a faja, and some doctors only recommend a stage 1 faja. Still, most women wear fajas after surgery (even if not recommended) because the compression aids in the relief of soreness. In any case, your surgeon should provide you with a stage 1 faja post surgery. This must be worn in combination with lipo foams, an abdominal board, and lumbar molder. Fajas provide compression which helps to reduce swelling, and reduce fluid buildup. They also help your skin to retract and reattach back to your muscles after liposuction.

The exact timeframe to switch from a stage 1 faja to a stage 2 faja varies depending on the policy of the doctor, and the healing rate of the patient. Some people switch as early as 1 week but usually, after about 2 weeks you should be able to switch to your stage 2 faja. Your stage 2 faja will provide more compression than a stage 1 faja. Moreover, it will help to mold and shape your body. Fajas come in a variety of knee length to ankle length, sleeved and sleeveless, and many more different styles to fit your convenience.

Lipo Foams

Lipo foams are a mandatory part of the healing process after liposuction. By flattening the skin evenly they help to reduce irregularities and help the skin to heal in a uniform fashion. Lipo foams provide additional compression, which helps to reduce swelling. Lipo foams also prevent the pain of your faja rubbing against your skin often referred to as a faja burn.

Ab Boards

Abdominal boards often referred to as ab boards, are used to provide additional compression to your abdominal area. They also help to rid your body of excess fluid in your abdominal region. Ab boards help to flatten your abdomen, and aid in providing a structure for the skin to use during reattachment.

Lumbar Molder

A lumbar molder is a triangular device which is placed in the lumbar region of the back when you wear your faja. It helps to give you that scoop in the back. It also defines the outline of the top portion of your buttocks. Remember, fat was just removed from these areas so it is important to mold it.

Vitamins and Supplements to Take

- Arnica tablets/ Arnica tea...aid in the relief of bruising and swelling
- Vitamin B12...helps bone marrow in forming new blood cells, and helps with energy production
- Vitamin C...speeds the healing of wounds
- Bromelain...speeds the recovery time, helps with inflammation, prevents blood clots, and helps digestion
- Calendula tea...prevents infection, promotes healing, and reduces scarring
- Stool softener...take occasionally to ensure you do not strain to move your bowels

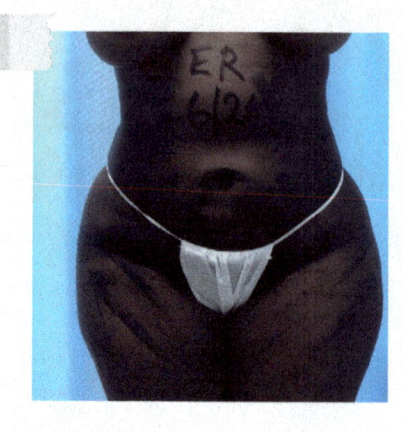
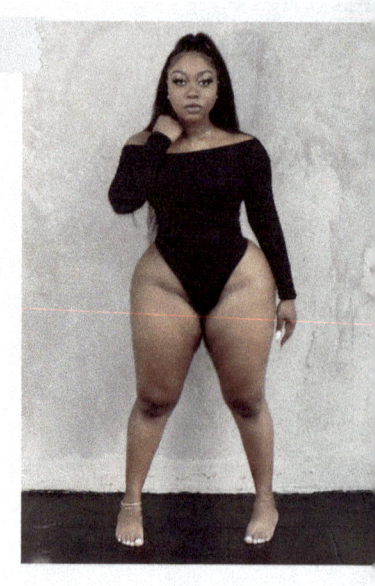
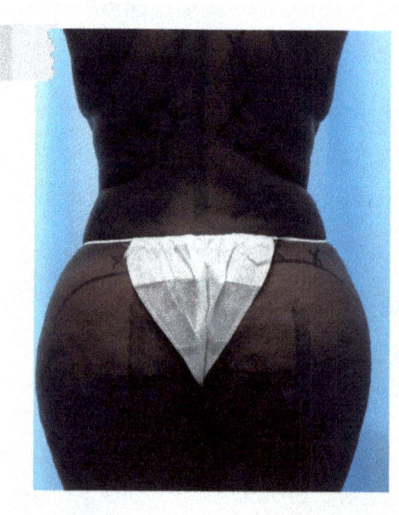

Before and after a BBL procedure with Dr.Dowbak of New Life Plastic Surgery in Miami, FL.

Laterals (Lats) v.s. Hips

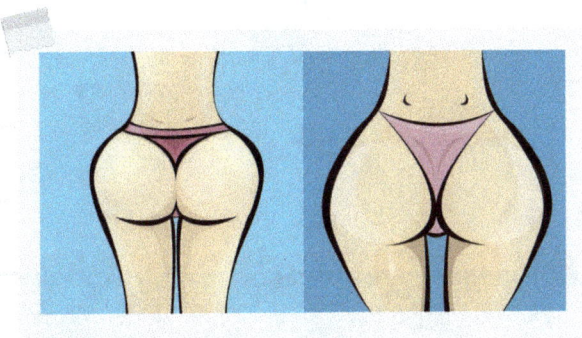

For "laterals"(left) fat is transferred higher in the hip area. This provides for a dramatic vixen-like appearance. For "hips"(right) fat is transferred lower in the hip area to provide a naturally curvy look.

Slope v.s. Shelf

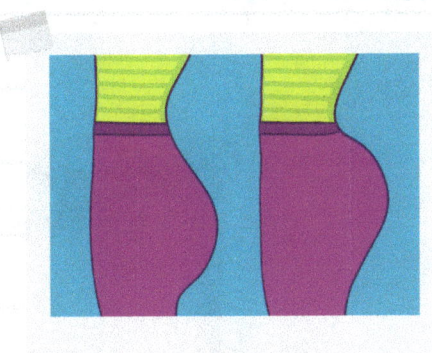

A "slope"(left) has more fat distributed towards the bottom of the buttocks, whereas a "shelf"(right) has more fat distributed in the upper region of the buttocks.

Healing rates/times may vary based on the individual. In order to aid your body in the healing process, you should follow your doctors instructions while also providing your body with the needed nutrients and ample amounts of rest.

First Days

The first 1-3 days after having liposuction is when it will be the most painful or uncomfortable (depending on your pain tolerance level). Some women compare the pain of liposuction to extreme soreness from the gym. Immediately after surgery you will probably just want to take your medication and get some rest. You may not have an appetite, so make sure you eat light foods and stay hydrated. You should be wearing your compression socks, stage 1 faja, lipo foams, ab board, and lumbar molder. These items should only be removed during washing times.

1 week

Within about a week of surgery you should be able to return to your normal routine with a few restrictions. However, you will still experience soreness and numbness in the areas affected by lipo. You will see differences in your body as swelling goes down, and your body goes through the fat survival process. You are no longer required to wear your compression socks.

1 month

As your body continues to heal you will begin to feel better day by day. You may notice changes in the contour of your body as the swelling continues to go down. Some patients begin wearing a waist trainer on top of their faja for additional compression. Although by now blood vessels should be grown into your newly grafted fat, you should still avoid putting direct pressure on the fat. You may start short walks as a form of exercise.

6 weeks

At this time, you may notice that you are back to feeling "normal". You may still have numbness in some areas where the lipo was performed, but you are getting more feeling back each day. By now, blood vessels should be fully grown into your new fat and pumping strong blood cells to your transferred fat. The shape of your butt will remain the same and you should not experience anymore volume/fat loss. It is now safe to sit normally without the use of a pressure offloading pillow. You may also increase your fitness regimen (with restrictions). Keep it at a comfortable pace and do not over exert yourself.

3 months

Congrats on reaching your third month mark! You will notice that swelling has gone down significantly and that you have started to get feeling back in the areas that have been lipoed. You no longer have to wear your stage 2 faja, although some patients continue to do so for better results. By this time, you are able to see your final BBL results. If you have any concerns or are unhappy with your results you should reach out to your doctor at this time. There are now no restrictions on training, and you may incorporate all levels of fitness into your routine.

6 months

As the months continue to go by you will see more improved results each day, especially if you incorporate some sort of fitness routine. Make sure you are helping to maintain your results by eating healthy. If you are considering a second round to achieve your desired look now is the time to start planning for that.

1 Year

By now your life has probably changed for the better. Not only do you physically look great but, you have a newfound confidence within yourself. You've started to look at things more positively and you are happy. Keep on shining!

Sitting Chart

Week 1

Sit only when using the bathroom (#2). Use female urinal for urinating.

Week 2

Sit when necessary with the use of a BBL or boppy pillow. Stand up every 15-30 minutes to shift your weight and keep the blood flowing.

Week 3

Sit when necessary with the use of a BBL or boppy pillow. Stand up every 30-60 minutes to shift your weight and keep the blood flowing.

Week 4

Sit when necessary with the use of a BBL or boppy pillow. Stand up every 1-2 hours to shift your weight and keep the blood flowing.

Week 5 — Sit normally with the use of BBL or boppy pillow.

Week 6 — Sit as usual, no pillow required.

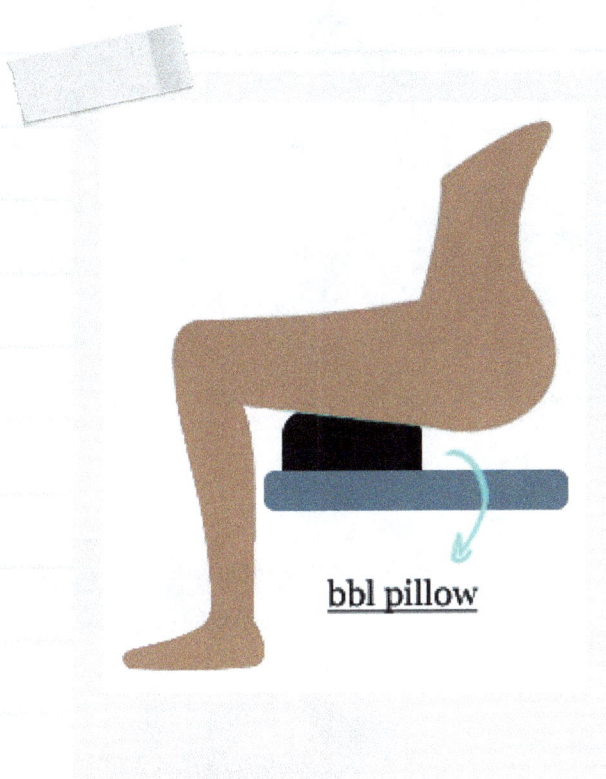

bbl pillow

What you will need

Your flight home should be one of comfort and convenience. Consider bringing a blanket, neck pillow, form of entertainment or other things to make your flight more bearable. All medications should be packed in your carry on. When booking your returning flight, look for a nonstop flight. If none are available, book the flight that has the least amount of connecting flights and layover time.

You will not be able to sit directly on your butt, so you will need to use a pillow (either a boppy pillow or a BBL pillow). The boppy pillow is most suitable for longer travel. Its cotton stuffing will provide more comfort vs. the styrofoam BBL pillow. It is suggested that you book a "wide" or "large" seat. This will ensure that you have enough space to place your pillow. You will not have to worry about your hips being squished or risk damaging the grafted fat. Since you will need to move around the plane to keep blood flowing and circulating, it is best to get an aisle seat. If it is within your budget to do so consider booking a seat in first class for your return, especially for international and longer flights.

Airport Check in

Your doctor should provide you with a few letters to make your departure as smooth as possible. Amongst those letters will be one stating that you recently had surgery. Show this to your agent upon checking in, and you will be provided an escort to assist you to your gate via wheelchair. The escort will also help you get through airport security faster. Once you get on the plane and get settled, you will also need to show that letter to a flight attendant so that they are aware that you just had surgery. Once the plane has reached its cruising altitude you will need to walk around in timed intervals (refer to sitting chart) to keep blood flowing to your newly transferred fat cells.

NAME:		D.O.B:	PHONE#:
Company Name & Address:	New Life Plastic Surgery 8400 SW 8 ST Miami FL 33144 info@newlifecosmetic.com 305-501-5020		Date of Procedure:

Flight Assistance Certificate

Duration of activity per day.	
Lifting Limitations & restrictions.	
Duration of standing Activity.	**Please allow patient to walk during flight as needed.**
Walking duration & restrictions.	
Seat activity & restrictions.	**Patient cannot be seated for a long period of time. When seated she will be using a special cushion.**
Driving Limits.	
Activities to be specifically avoided.	
Others.	**Please Assist patient with luggage as needed.**
COMMENTS & NOTES:	
DR. NAME:	Gregory Dowbak M.D.

In order to maintain your results, it is best to combine a combination of eating healthy and working out. Below is an example of a suggested meal plan for a week's worth of clean eating. Based on your preferred lifestyle and dieting choices (meat lovers, vegetarian, vegan, pescatarian, keto etc.), incorporate the types of things that you normally eat into balanced meals. This will help you to tailor your meal plan.

	BREAKFAST	LUNCH	SNACKS	DINNER
MONDAY	Greens Smoothie	Meal prepped meal	Fresh Fruit	Salad
TUESDAY	Greens Smoothie	Salad	Advocado with Salt & Pepper	Meal prepped meal
WEDNESDAY	Fruit Smoothie	Meal prepped meal	Greek Yogurt with Berries	Salad
THURSDSAY	Greens Smoothie	Salad	Cheat Snack	Meal prepped meal
FRIDAY	Greens Smoothie	Meal prepped meal	Fresh Fruit	Salad
SATURDAY	Fruit Smoothie	Salad	1 Rice Cake	Meal prepped meal
SUNDAY	Greens Smoothie	Cheat Meal	Cucumber Salad	Salad

Things To Consider

- After regular liposuction you may have loose skin. To avoid this it is best to combine lipo with some sort of skin tightening procedure such as J-plasma. There are also various types of liposuction such as Laser, HD, and Ultrasound, which can help prevent sagging skin post op.

- Some women experience back pain after receiving a BBL (even after a full recovery).

- You can still gain weight after liposuction so try your best to eat healthy and exercise often in order to maintain your results.

- After liposuction the shape of your belly button my change.

Tips

- Drinking alcohol too soon after surgery will significantly slow down your recovery. Most doctors will advise you to stop consuming alcohol at least two weeks before your surgery up unto two weeks afterwards. To be on the safe side, it is best to wait until you have fully recovered.

- Within the first week of recovery you may get lightheaded when standing even for short periods of time. Be sure to keep Gatorade, Powerade or electrolyte water nearby even when you shower and stay hydrated!

- Let someone assist you with showering at least for the first couple of days after your procedure.

- Use cold water to clean blood out of your faja.

- Wait approximately 8 weeks before wearing jeans or tight fitting clothing.

Q) How long should I stay in town after surgery?

A) Each surgeon has different requirements for out of town patients. Consult with them ahead of time and let them know if you can only stay for a certain timeframe.

Q) How long is the full recovery period after a BBL?

A) Most people are able to return to work within 2-3 weeks. Some return as early as 1 week post op. However, the full recovery time is around 6 months to one year. Ultimately, the rate of recovery varies per individual.

Q) When will I be able to sit again?

A) Please refer to the sitting chart in this book.

Q) How much does a BBL cost?

A) BBL's vary in price depending on the location and fame of the surgeon. However, they can range anywhere from $3500 to $16000. You may want to start saving approximately $7500 as this seems to be the average cost.

Q) How do I find a good doctor?

A) A doctor who is board certified and puts the safety of the patient first is a great doctor! Use some of the tools mentioned in this book to find doctors in a specific area and view their work.

Q) Why am I itching ?

A) After liposuction, there will be some itching as swelling subsides and your skin reattaches to the muscle. This is also a sign that your nerves are waking up. You can use an anti-itch cream to combat any discomfort from the itching.

Q) Are there scars after a bbl?

A) After liposuction there will be minimal scarring at the incision sites. These scars usually fade and lighten overtime with age and the aid of some sort of gel/cream agent.

Q) Will my butt move after a BBL?

A) Yes! Once the transferred fat fully grafts to your body and the swelling subsides it is just like any other fat. Get out there and shake that thang.

Q) What is the fluff stage?

A) In a couple of months your swelling will be fully gone and your fat will soften up and become more "jiggly". At this stage the butt may also appear larger as swelling in the flanks and torso is now gone. This is often referred to as the fluff stage. Some people refer to this as a visit from the fluff fairy.

CERTIFICATE OF COMPLETION

THIS CERTIFIES THAT

has succesfully completed the BBL Basics course, and is now a bbl expert!

Egypt Rodriguez
INSTRUCTOR

BBL Basics